NO NOT TOO TIGHT, 'JUST RIGHT'

(Tuning the Mind)

by Swamini Vimalananda

Central Chinmaya Mission Trust

•

Reprint till - December 2011 - 22,000 copies
Revised Edition – February 2014 - 4,000 copies

•

Published by:
Chinmaya Prakashan
The Publications Division of
Central Chinmaya Mission Trust
Sandeepany Sadhanalaya
Saki Vihar Road, Mumbai 400072, India
Tel.: +91-22-2857 2367, 2857 5806 Fax: +91-22-2857 3065
Email: ccmtpublications@chinmayamission.com
Website: www.chinmayamission.com

•

Distribution Centre in USA:
Chinmaya Mission West
Publications Division, 560 Bridgetown Pike
Langhorne, PA 19053, USA
Tel.: 1-888-CMW-READ, (215) 396-0390 Fax: (215) 396-9710
Email: publications@chinmayamission.org
Website: www.chinmayapublications.org

•

Illustrated by: Shri Romesh Malhotra

•

Price: ₹ 50/-

•

Printed by:
Usha Multigraphs Pvt. Ltd., Mumbai - 13, Tel.: 2492 5354

•

ISBN 978-81-7597-627-6

Acknowledgement

I have talked to hundreds of children and given demonstrations on Value Education based on the topic of this book. The response was overwhelming each time. Thus sprang the thought of putting it together into a ready reckoner of self-improvement.

I was encouraged to print it by Radhika Krishnakumar, who not only edited it but also gave many constructive suggestions to fine-tune it. Were it not for her perseverance, this book would not have come out. Mytrae Maganti came in to proofread it. Shivakumar was continuously on the job of putting the book together. On seeing the manuscript Suresh Wadhwani readily came forward to sponsor the first edition. Grateful thanks to them.

Many thanks to Shri. Romesh Malhotra for the lovely illustrations which he did as his '*sevā*' to the cause.

The concepts are from the *Bhagavad-gītā* and the title and idea evolved from a talk by Pūjya Gurujī Swami Tejomayanandajī that I heard many years ago at a children's camp. My humble *praṇāmas* to him.

DEDICATED TO

The One ...

Who makes it all ...

possible and worthwhile.

Transliteration and Pronunciation Guide

In the book, Devanāgarī characters are transliterated according to the scheme adopted by the International Congress of Orientalists at Athens in 1912. In it one fixed pronunciation value is given to each letter; f, q, w, x and z are not called to use. An audio recording of this guide is available at http://chinmayamission.com/scriptures.php. According to this scheme:

Devanāgarī	Translit-eration	Sounds Like	Devanāgarī	Translit-eration	Sounds Like
अ	a	son	ढ्	ḍh	adhesive*
आ	ā	father	ण्	ṇ	under*
इ	i	different	त्	t	tabla
ई	ī	feel	थ्	th	thumb
उ	u	full	द्	ḋ	this
ऊ	ū	boot	ध्	ḋh	Gandhi
ऋ	ṛ	rhythm*	न्	n	nose
ॠ	ṝ	**	प्	p	pen
ऌ	ḷ	**	फ्	ph	phantom*
ए	e	evade	ब्	b	boil
ऐ	ai	delight	भ्	bh	abhor
ओ	o	core	म्	m	mind
औ	au	now	य्	y	yes
क्	k	calm	र्	r	right
ख्	kh	khan	ल्	l	love
ग्	g	gate	व्	v	very
घ्	gh	ghost	श्	ś	shut
ङ्	ṅ	ankle*	ष्	ṣ	sugar
च्	c	chuckle	स्	s	simple
छ्	ch	witch*	ह्	h	happy
ज्	j	justice	ं	ṁ	improvise
झ्	jh	Jhansi	ः	ḥ	**
ञ्	ñ	banyan	क्ष्	kṣ	action
ट्	ṭ	tank	त्र्	tr	three*
ठ्	ṭh	**	ज्ञ्	jñ	gnosis
ड्	ḍ	dog	ऽ	'	a silent 'a'

* These letters don't have an exact English equivalent. An approximation is given here.
** These sounds cannot be approximated in English words.

Contents

Introduction

Every effect must have a cause. It naturally follows that the world we experience must also have a cause. There are various causes for the various objects, phenomena, circumstances and experiences of the world. For example, a seed gives rise to a tree, condensation causes rain, unfulfilled desires cause frustration and anger and so on. There may be one or many causes for a phenomenon. For example, India won a cricket match because of good fielding, good bowling and indifferent batting by its opponents. But what is the ultimate Cause – the Cause of all causes – the cause of the entire world and not just a small part or event of it? Both science and religion seek this ultimate Cause.

Logically thinking, an object, energy or phenomenon of the world cannot be the ultimate Cause of the world since:

1. A part cannot create the whole. The finite cannot create the infinite.

2. Any object being a part of the world cannot itself be the cause of the world.

3. The cause has to precede the effect. The object would have to exist before the world came into being and yet all objects are logically a part of creation.

These and many other logical fallacies would occur if we assume that an object, form of energy or phenomenon is the ultimate Cause of the world. Therefore the ultimate Cause cannot be an object or an aspect of the world. Then, what is it?

Let us first see what the world is. Then we can arrive at its cause by negating all that the world represents. The creation, universe or world is names for forms with attributes, which exist within the realm of time and space. Therefore, the ultimate Cause of the creation must be a nameless, formless, qualityless, timeless and spaceless entity. It is called God in religion and Truth in philosophy.

This Truth (Puruṣa or Brahman) has the unmanifest infinite potential (prakṛti) to create the vast universe. This potential first manifests as the five subtle elements (tanmātrās): space (ākāśa), air (vāyu), fire (agni), water (jala) and the earth (pṛthivī). The elements are called subtle because they cannot be perceived by our sense organs. These subtle elements form the entire subtle world of our thoughts, emotions, talents and abilities. They then grossify to form the five gross elements. These form the gross world that we perceive with our five sense organs (eyes, ears, nose, skin, and tongue) as forms, sounds, smells, touch and taste.

If everything has emerged from the same Truth, the same unmanifest potential, the same subtle and gross elements, then why do we perceive differences? Why is one brilliant and another dull?

Prakṛti, the unmanifest potential, inherently has three qualities. These manifest in various ways causing a wide range of differences. For example, tea contains milk, sugar and tea powder. The various permutations and combinations of these three ingredients create a variety of tastes. Similarly, everyone and everything in the creation is made up of three qualities (guṇas):

sattva, rajas and tamas. The permutations and combinations of these three create the vast variety in the world.

The main characteristic of sattva-guṇa is knowledge (jñāna). Other characteristics are compassion, faith, love, self-control, understanding, purity, equanimity and memory. The main characteristic of rajo-guṇa is activity (pravṛtti). Other characteristics are ambition, dynamism, restlessness, haste, anger, jealousy, greed and passion. The main characteristic of tamo-guṇa is inertia (jaḍatva). Other characteristics are disorganised thinking or behaviour, carelessness, laziness, forgetfulness, violence and criminal thoughts.

The cause pervades the effect. Hence, these three qualities of prakṛti pervade everything in the creation. However, when one quality is predominant, the other two lie dormant. The inert world of objects is predominantly tāmasika. Plants manifest more rajo-guṇa than stones do, and animals even more than plants. Man can manifest sattva-guṇa to a greater extent than animals, and presiding deities (devatās) even more than man. Even amongst plants, flowers, trees, animals and birds, some are sāttvika, others rājasika and yet others tāmasika. The tulsī, lotus, pīpal (banyan), cow and swan are seen to be more sāttvika and are, therefore, worshipped in India. The pitcher plant, sunflower, mango tree, monkey and crow are more rājasika whereas weeds or cacti, babul, the buffalo and the vulture are more tāmasika. Look around at the world and try to see these guṇas in the beings around you.

Human beings too have these three guṇas. Different qualities gain dominance at different times, but one of them generally dominates each personality. Hence, we may categorise people as sāttvika (sattva-dominant) rājasika (rajas-dominant) and tāmasika (tamas-dominant). Remember everything we do – the way we sit, eat, walk, talk, work or behave – reflects the quality or mood of the mind. For example, in a sāttvika mood we eat unhurriedly and neatly; in a rājasika mood hurriedly and barely chewing; while in a tāmasika mood in a sloppy and lethargic manner.

What do we want to be? What is the ideal combination of the guṇas we should strive to have?

When the strings of a sitāra (or any other stringed instrument) are too loose, they produce a base and unmusical sound. If they are too tight, they make a squeaky or shrill sound. But when they are tuned right, they produce melodious music. Similarly, if the strings of our mind are too loose (tamo-guṇa-dominant) we are dull, lazy and often negative in our thoughts. If they are too tight (rajo-guṇa-dominant) then despite being ambitious and hard working, we are often tense, worried and unhappy. But when the strings of our minds are tuned right (sattva-guṇa-dominant) then we are poised, successful and happy – there is beautiful music in our lives. Therefore, the formula for success and happiness is – **'Not too loose, not too tight, JUST RIGHT.'**

When I look at a mirror and see dirt on my face, I wash it off. I enhance my looks by highlighting my good features (guṇa ādhāna) and reducing or managing its defects (doṣa apanayana). This book is like a pocket-size mirror. The 23 aspects expounded herein are meant to help us look at ourselves and guide us to beautify our inner selves and lives.

1. Vision (dṛṣṭi)

'Yathā dṛṣṭi, tathā sṛṣṭi': As our vision, so the world appears to us. For example, when we like a person, we see only the good in him but when we do not like a person, nothing he does pleases us.

Sāttvika: It is a 'holistic vision' which enables us to see the role of various parts and aspects as within the realm of the totality. This helps us give each aspect of life its due importance. For instance, if we want to be happy, we must be aware that a healthy mind is as important as a healthy body. This vision enables us to see unity in diversity (abheda dṛṣṭi), such as 'all Indians are my brothers and sisters' or 'the whole world is my family' (vasudhaiva kuṭumbakam). This vision enables man to appreciate the common cause behind various effects. Take the example of a doctor who diagnoses the cause of a disease while examining its symptoms, or a scientist who discovers the cause behind

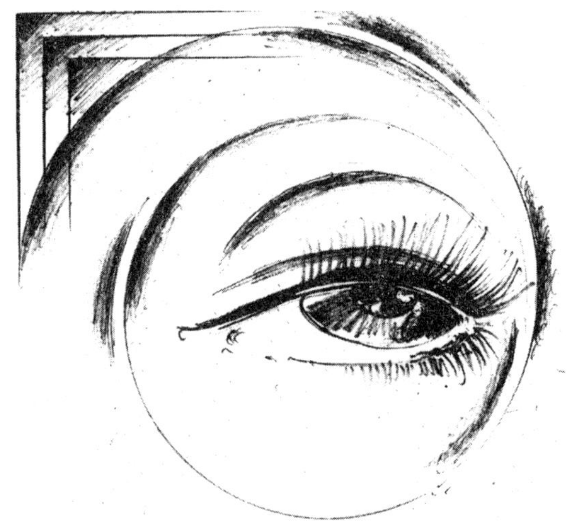

a chemical reaction. When man is able to see the essential commonness even while perceiving and responding to the differences in the creation, he learns to identify with others and loves and serves all selflessly. This idea becomes clear with a few examples. Seeing the common factor 'I' in all parts of the body, I love each part equally and serve my entire body spontaneously. Lokamānya Tilak, the great freedom fighter, on receiving news of his wife's death, while at prison, was able to say, "Presently, I have no time for personal sorrow. My country's sorrow is my sorrow", because he identified himself with the entire nation. Saints realise the Truth that "the 'Self' (Divinity) in me is the 'Self' (Divinity) in all", and therefore love all as themselves. For example, Śrī Ramakrishna Paramahamsa viewed even a prostitute as the Divine Mother and prostrated at her feet.

Rājasika: It is a 'partial vision' wherein certain parts or effects are given undue importance. In addition, the whole or totality is mistaken for the part. For example:

- Becoming a doctor or pursuing a particular profession is the goal of one's life.
- Comforts are more important than relationships.
- It is enough to be religious once in a while.
- It is more important to look good than to be good.

Rājasika vision gives importance and reality only to the differences (bheda dṛṣṭi), thereby creating divisions within the family, society and country. For instance, the British vision was 'divide and rule' which caused the partition of India. Sāttvika vision makes us share and care whereas rājasika vision, as in the previous example, separates, breaks up and categorises people and things based on 'me' and 'mine' versus 'you' and 'yours'. Marriages and joint families have broken up due to rājasika vision. With such a vision, one becomes petty and quarrelsome and his or her mind remains engrossed only in certain aspects of life causing a lopsided development and growth, both within and without.

Tāmasika: Such a vision makes man mistake the 'part' to be the whole or totality, the effect to be the cause and the means to be the goal. This is more because of insensitivity and ignorance than out of self-centredness as is the case with rājasika vision. Such a person's mind is unable to conceive of the whole, thus he or she becomes narrow-minded (alpa dṛṣṭi), illogical, unreasonable and fanatic about beliefs. For example, a tāmasika vision gives rise to statements like "My God alone saves", "There is no God", "Money is God" or "Money is everything in life". Or, one in love says, "You are my life. Without you, I am nothing." Such people cannot unfold or progress in life as their minds are closed to new ideas and creative or progressive thoughts. For instance, even in this day, there are some who claim that women should not be educated and that men are superior to women.

2. Actions (karma) – Undertaking

Action is the insignia of life – man cannot live without actions. Actions by themselves are neither good nor bad. It is the intentions behind them that make them good or bad. For example, when a doctor performs a surgery, it is not called murder even if the patient dies in the process.

All undertakings in life may be categorised as sāttvika, rājasika or tāmasika depending on the thought (intentions or motives) behind them.

Sāttvika: Proper and deep thought behind an action makes it a sāttvika undertaking. One thinks about the goal behind the action, the consequences and the results of the action. For example, 'If I take a bribe, it may bring me some easy money but it will certainly set a bad example for my children'. One also thinks about the time, effort, money, manpower and material required for an

undertaking. For instance, 'How many hours do I need to study each subject to prepare well for my exams?' One also prioritises one's goals – 'At this time in life, studying is more important than partying.' Man also thinks about the harm that could be caused to others either while doing an action or as a result of it, and whether it is worth doing or worthy of being done. For example, 'Should I kill the cow which is worshipped in India just to pamper my tongue? Will this not hurt the feelings of my mother who feeds her daily?' Swami Chinmayanandajī said, "Plan out your work and then work out your plan." After planning well, when one's all energy is focused on one's actions, he or she becomes efficient and successful.

Rājasika: Incomplete and distracted thinking makes an undertaking rājasika. Actions based on immature thinking, half-baked plans and sentimental promptings often prove fruitless. For example, 'I voted for 'X' in the elections because he is good-looking'. When many goals are attempted to be reached simultaneously, none gets satisfactorily fulfilled. An example is studying and watching T.V. at the same time. One becomes a 'Jack of all trades and master of none'. Due to lack of proper thinking, there is unnecessary delay, disorganised effort and tension during actions.

Tāmasika: Rash, whimsical, indiscriminative, impulsive and mindless undertakings are tāmasika. Some examples are 'I spoke thoughtlessly', 'I gave up engineering because I did not like the teacher' or 'I applied for the job because it is my hobby to attend interviews'. Some act in haste and repent at leisure. Others act driven by strong emotions. Such actions most often cause only guilt, regret and misery.

3. Actions (kartavya) – Inherent Tendencies and Duties

Each of us has inherent tendencies, potential talents and abilities which are called our svadharma. For example, Arjuna's gift or svadharma was brilliance in archery.

Also, depending on one's stage and position in life, duties come to us unasked. If I am a student, I have to study, whether I like it or not! These are called viśeṣa dharma or kartavya. Actions with respect to our inherent talents and duties can be sāttvika, rājasika or tāmasika.

Sāttvika: To act according to one's inherent abilities, thereby manifesting one's full inner potential, is to follow one's svadharma. In such cases, one progresses easily like a fish taking to water. For instance, a man

with acute business acumen prospers rapidly whereas another without the flair for business, even if loaded with business management degrees, may fail. Man easily becomes proficient (skilled knowledge-wise) and efficient (skilled application-wise) in his svadharma. Work becomes a joy and he works tirelessly and rapidly, progressing within and without. A father once told his son, "Son, take a job that you love and you will not have to labour any day of your life!"

A sāttvika person does his or her duties cheerfully, without expecting others to congratulate, appreciate or reward him or her. This is most beautifully seen in the mother who serves her child without expectation. There is joy in the very performance of the duty and in doing it well which results in deep satisfaction during and upon completion of the task. Even unpleasant duties are done without complaining but with the attitude that it is the right thing to do and that it has to be done, such as escorting a senile, old relative to the hospital. A sāttvika person is ever alert (tatpara) in the performance of his or her duties and does them properly, efficiently and without pride (anahaṁvādī), pomp or show, like Gandhijī who washed the bathrooms in his āśrama. We have a duty towards our family, society, nation and universe. We also have a duty towards ourselves. A sāttvika person is aware and ready to perform all his duties without any confusion in priorities. For example, when the country is being attacked, my first duty is towards the nation and not just my family. A sāttvika person does his work with patience and enthusiasm, in true sportsman spirit, and is therefore never elated or dejected in success or failure. He maintains his equipoise at all times. Jaṭāyu fought Rāvaṇa till death and even as he lay defeated and dying, he had no regrets.

Rājasika: When a person does work that is not in consonance with his or her inherent nature (aptitude), such work is called paradharma. For example, many who have no inclination to serve and sacrifice become doctors, only to make money. For such people, there is little joy in their work as the result is the main focus. Therefore, the work itself becomes tedious, boring, burdensome and full of tension. Also, unethical methods may be employed in the process as when Rāvaṇa disguised himself as a sannyāsī to abduct Sītā. Some act only to impress others like one who sits in meditation to appear spiritual. Others blindly copy peers in enrolling for a professional course because all their friends have done so. There is no inner unfoldment or fulfilment in such actions – often these lead to unhealthy competition, jealousy, frustration, depression or dejection.

The rājasika person does his or her duties with expectations(karma-phala-prepsā) attachment (rāga) and pride (ahaṁvāda). We often hear statements like 'My relations must appreciate what I do for them' or 'Without me, this house will never run well'. Such a person is often worried, tense, fearful and filled with thoughts like 'I have to get my daughter married. What will happen if we cannot find a groom for her?', 'What if I fail in my exams?' and many other negative mental projections. Such a person is confused about his or her duties and gets distracted by temptations even while doing them. Examples are those of a student watching a movie the day before an exam. or of Arjuna who was confused on the

Kurukshetra battlefield as to what he should do. The rājasika person is not able to maintain his mental equipoise because of his attitude towards action.

Tāmasika: All of us have good and bad in us. The tāmasika person performs actions based on his baser values (adharma). Violent tendencies make him resort to terrorism, murder and the like. Such actions give him no joy, and in the long run, his life becomes a hell. A tāmasika person does not do what he should do (kartavya karma) and does what he should not do (niṣiddha karma). He is lazy (ālasya), postpones and forgets things easily (pramāda). He prefers inaction to action and finds excuses for not doing things. Such people stagnate and rot in life. Swami Chinmayanandajī said, 'If you rest, you rust.' Such people are burdened by the guilt of not doing what has to be done, or doing the wrong things and they tend to find various means of escape such as drugs or alcohol. They also keep relegating their duties to others. Such people become a burden to society – they do not mind living off others' sweat and toil and even feel it their right to be taken care of by others. Even their efforts are half-hearted and their minds disintegrated (ayukta). It takes them a week to do what can be done in a day (dīrghasūtrī) and they are often dissatisfied and depressed (viṣāda). They believe in the philosophy of 'chalta hai' and 'hota hai' – even if the work is not done, they tell themselves, 'It is alright' and 'Don't worry, it will get done by someone at some unspecified time.'

4. Intellect (buddhi)

Man's intellect has a very important role to play in his or her life. It is the driver of our life (buddhiṁ tu sārathi viddhi) and can lead us to great heights or to our downfall. It has the ability to observe, discriminate, understand, analyse, judge and decide what should be done in a given situation. It can be sāttvika, rājasika or tāmasika.

Sāttvika: The sāttvika intellect can figure out clearly, correctly and promptly what should be done and what should not be done under all circumstances. For example, 'I should not drink hot coffee after ice cream. It will disagree with my system.' It also knows what is right and wrong. For example, 'I must not copy in exams even if all around me do so'. It tells me what my duty is and what it is not. For instance, 'I must hand over the thief to the police. I need not beat him up to punish him'. It tells me what I should not

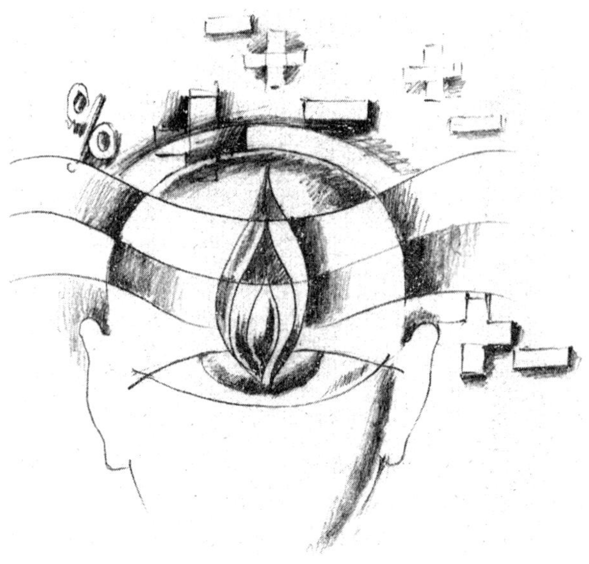

fear and warns me about what I should. For example, 'Since I speak the truth, I need not fear' or 'If I lie, I will get exposed'. The sāttvika intellect helps me understand what will cause bondage and sorrow and what will give lasting joy and freedom. For example, 'Attachments will cause sorrow. I should stay away from this person' or 'Living a disciplined life is good for me and will make me happy even though it is difficult'. The *Gītā* advises, 'Take refuge in your sāttvika intellect' (buddhou śaraṇam-anviccha) – it will lead you to glory and success.

Rājasika: The rājasika intellect gets easily confused, is vague at times, fluctuates in moods and thoughts and is, therefore, indecisive. Arjuna was confused on the battlefield – 'Should I fight or not? I can't decide.' Such people change their decisions often and doubt their decisions all the time.

Their actions are, therefore, not focused and their minds agitated and worried. For instance, 'I should not have joined the Engineering course but done a Catering course instead'. Some people are very good at deciding what others should do. In that their intellect is sāttvika but when it comes to making decisions in their own lives, they get confused (para upadeśe pāṇḍityam). They become good consultants, in solving others' problems. A rājasika intellect is undecided about most things in life. An actress was asked if she believed in astrology. "I believe in everything a little bit!" she replied.

Tāmasika: The tāmasika intellect either does not understand at all or misunderstands people or situations and, therefore, comes to wrong conclusions. For instance, a teacher was demonstrating the harmful effects of alcohol. A student, after seeing how worms died in a glass of alcohol, concluded, 'When we have worms in the stomach, we must drink alcohol!' Such an intellect views wrong to be right and prompts man into sinful acts. For example, 'Might is right, so I will bully everyone,' or 'All work and no play makes Jack a dull boy, so I will never work, just enjoy'.

5. Patience and Will (dhṛti)

To gain everything in life, patience, forbearance and will are most essential. These may be sāttvika, rājasika or tāmasika.

Sāttvika: Sāttvika patience is not patience in facing a particular situation but exists at all times, with everyone and under all circumstances. It enables man to consistently (avyabhicāriṇi) apply his or her body and mind to the task at hand until it is accomplished, like a man who makes it to the top of a mountain peak, even when physically exhausted. It helps man overcome adverse situations or obstacles that may arise while doing a task. His

will and patie
distracted, deje
they give him gr
more he is challeng
of Robert Bruce an

finally succeeded. 'Try, try ucceed' is the secret behind many achievements. We fell a hundred nes before we learned how to walk. If we had become impatient and given up, we would be crawling on our fours even today! A strong will can make the impossible possible. Śrī Buddha decided that he would not get up from under the bodhi tree till he attained realisation, even if he were to die in the process (śarīraṁ vā pātayāmi, kāryaṁ vā sādhayāmi). Man also needs patience with his own mental and physical shortcomings. For instance, one has to patiently cajole the mind to still it in meditation. One needs a great deal of forbearance and restraint in dealing with others, especially in situations like teaching a mentally handicapped child or house-training a dog. When one realises that whatever comes in life will also go, one learns not to get too attached to the good things of life or be impatient with difficult people and situations.

Rājasika: Patience, forbearance or will periodically shown towards some people or to accomplish some task (prasaṅgeṇa) is rājasika. A classic example is that of one who demonstrates remarkable patience with his boss but impatience with his wife. Some study or work patiently till the exam or project is over. Yet, once the task is accomplished, they go back to their normal impatient selves and lose their will, restraint or forbearance. Haven't we seen some who fast on Monday and feast on Tuesday? Some are patient till obstacles come their way. Then they lose their cool and either give up, get irritated or quickly frustrated. Statements such as 'How long will I have to bear the pain? I cannot take it anymore' amply demonstrate this.

Tāmasika: Tāmasika patience or will is to stubbornly hold on to a wrong notion or course of action. For example, 'I refuse to become happy', 'It is my opinion and I will not give it up even if proved wrong' or 'What if I die drinking? After all it is my life and I can do what I want with it.' A postman almost got hit by a charging bull while taking a short cut on the way to his work place. A passerby who saw this remarked that he just saved his skin by the teeth. The postman said, 'Yes, he almost gets me every day.' Some become neurotic in their thinking and actions, like when they assume, 'The whole world is after me'. Some live in the past, waste time daydreaming or live in a fool's paradise, and refuse to face the world.

6. Happiness (sukha)

All of us, without exception, want happiness in life. Each of us wants the maximum possible happiness. We feel that different objects, beings or circumstances are 'joy-giving' and hence, we adopt different pursuits. The quality of happiness we experience is sāttvika, rājasika or tāmasika.

Sāttvika: When our vision, actions, intellect and will are sāttvika, we experience sāttvika joy. A sāttvika mind is naturally and effortlessly cheerful, peaceful and poised. There is a sense of well-being, a feeling that life is beautiful and that living is a joy. The joy that results from dispassion, self-control, discipline, concentration, selflessness or doing good is sāttvika in nature. The sense of satisfaction that one gets in doing a job well, achieving something by one's own efforts, creating a piece of art, discovering something, understanding a subtle subject or

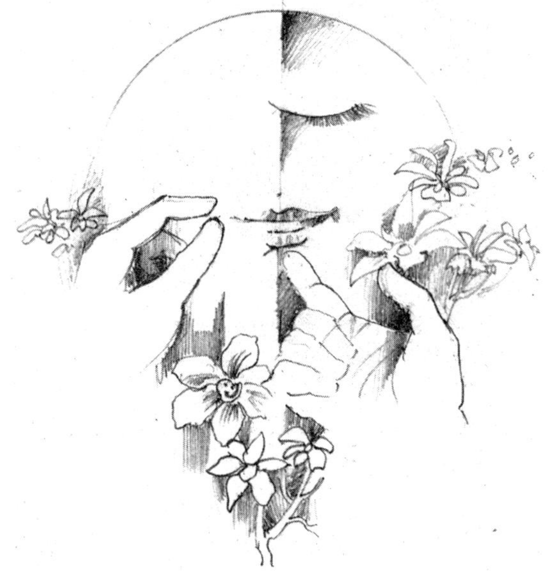

mastering a skill is sāttvika in nature. What may initially seem difficult and unattractive but which results in one's well-being and gives lasting joy is sāttvika. Classic examples are waking early, practising meditation or memorising arithmetic tables. Sāttvika joy can be effortlessly gained from simple things in life like sharing a heartfelt smile, watching the sun rise, good health, breathing fresh air, watching the flight of a bird or seeing the smile of an infant. Being with nature makes the mind restful, peaceful and gives sāttvika joy. A sensitive mind and keen senses have the capacity to gain sāttvika joy and acquire a taste for it. Sāttvika joy is subtle, yet its bondage is also subtle. One can get hooked on to subtle sense pleasures, which later cause sorrow.

Rājasika: When our vision, intellect and actions are rājasika, we experience rājasika joy. A rājasika mind has a taste for grosser joys. It seeks thrills and excitement from objects and beings like listening to fast music, watching 'thrillers' or partying. The joy we get from indulgence and comforts is rājasika. It depends on the coming together of various factors like the availability of the desired object, a healthy body and senses and the right mood or conducive environment. After all these factors come together, we experience a momentary joy which leaves a craving for more of the same or gives rise to new desires within. Having enjoyed a holiday in Ooty, many want to repeatedly return to the same place or visit Kodaikkanal and Munnar. In case one or more of the factors do not come together, we do not experience joy, rather we feel angry or dejected. Take this typical instance – with much effort we gather our friends, reach the movie theatre, procure tickets in the black market and sit for a popular movie. Suddenly, half-way through the movie, the power supply goes off and you have to return home. Imagine the feeling. If the joy is not to our expectation, then there is disappointment and dissatisfaction. If the early morning tea is lukewarm, then some feel that the entire day has had a lukewarm start. All the problems of that day are blamed on the tea. Rājasika pursuits seem very attractive and easy to get joys are experienced but they result in the exhaustion of the mind, dullening of the senses, money being 'blown' and yet do not give much satisfaction to the intellect. Do recall an unwanted shopping spree, late night partying or eating at a marriage feast? A mind that gets habituated to pleasure seeking can hardly entertain noble or great thoughts.

Tāmasika: Tāmasika vision, actions and intellect give rise to tāmasika joy. It is the joy that makes it very difficult to get up from bed each morning and that one gets by lying around in bed even after waking up. A tāmasika mind revels in laziness, sleep, sadistic and masochistic pleasures, harming and hurting others, vulgarity, drugs and alcohol. Such people feel that ignorance is bliss. Some even take to murder, rape, revenge, loot and plunder. This is a base joy and appeals only to our lower instincts.

7. Sleep

Sleep is basically a tāmasika activity. But the quality of one's sleep can be sāttvika, rājasika or tāmasika depending on how you sleep and awake.

Sāttvika: When we enjoy sound sleep and awake alert, rested, rejuvenated, bright and refreshed, then that sleep is sāttvika. It fosters a creative, contemplative mood and gives a good start to the day. About six to seven hours of good sleep at night is enough to refresh a normally healthy person.

Rājasika: When our sleep is restless and interrupted by spells of wakefulness or dreams, it indicates rājasika sleep. The body feels tired and the mind is agitated upon waking. We tend to get irritated quickly, which is obviously not a good way to start the day.

Tāmasika: When we experience heavy sleep, and wake up feeling lethargic, dull and heavy, sleep is tāmasika. We linger in bed even after waking up, and the first thought on waking up is to go back to sleep. It gives a very dull start to the day.

8. The Powers of the Mind

The mind has many powers. We will now explore how the three guṇas or qualities act through the powers of the mind.

1. The Veiling Power (āvaraṇa śakti): Tamo-guṇa has the power to veil or hide that which exists and block our thinking capacity. It either totally incapacitates our discrimination power ('I don't know, I don't understand, I can't think') or sets it thinking in a wrong direction. It creates a resistance to any form of physical or mental activity such as, 'I don't want to know' or 'I want to sleep on and on'. It is the power of inertia that induces man to want to remain in a state of motion or rest without change.

2. The Projection Power (vikṣepa śakti): Rajo-guṇa has the power to project, create, act, interact and change. It projects even that which is not there and creates illusions which seem very real. It starts its work of

creating false illusions once tamo-guṇa has done its work of hiding the Truth. For instance, not knowing the object lying in the dark to be a rope, we mistake it for a snake and get frightened by it. Not really knowing a person, we assume he or she is not good. Man acts and reacts in the world based on his or her subjective projections, prejudices and the colourings of the mind. These make him or her agitated and miserable. Projecting happiness on an object, we run after it and turn away disappointed when it fails to make us happy. The projections of the human mind are unending and infinite.

3. Discrimination Power (viveka śakti): Sattva-guṇa has the power to discriminate and helps us to see ourselves and the world 'as it is', without veiling or projections. Think about the following statements:

a) On observing closely with a calm mind, one sees the rope, thereby dispelling the false vision of the snake and the fear due to it.

b) Through experience one understands that no object really makes us happy or unhappy, but it is our mind's projections that cause these emotions.

9. Sense Organs (indriya)

The innumerable objects of the world are perceived by us as sounds (śabda), touch (sparśa), forms and colours (rūpa), taste (rasa) and smells (gandha) through the five sense organs: the ability to hear (śrotra-indriya), the ability to feel (sparśa-indriya), the ability to see (cakṣu-indriya), the ability to taste (rasa-indriya) and the ability to smell (ghrāṇa-indriya) respectively. Prompted by the mind, these senses perceive the world through the outer instruments (golaka): ears, skin, eyes, tongue and nose. For every sense organ the mind has its own likes and dislikes. 'I like the smell of a rose', 'I dislike cheese', 'I love rock music' and so on. The quality of our perceptions makes the senses sāttvika, rājasika or tāmasika.

Sāttvika: When our perceptions are keen, sensitive and focused, our senses are said to be sāttvika. A village child is able to focus on far off sounds effortlessly and interpret them correctly. A wine taster is able to distinguish

or identify the quality of wine with a sip or just by smelling the drink. Keen, sensitive and clear perceptions add to the joy of man. For instance, watching the wonderful colours in nature and feeling a fresh, cool breeze certainly makes one exhilarated.

Rājasika: When our perceptions are unfocused, confused and vague and our senses tired, they are said to be rājasika. An indulgent child who is overfed on chocolates has no more a keen taste to enjoy them. Eyes that watch too much T.V. are tired and dull.

Tāmasika: When our perceptions are slow and the senses dullened by disuse or abuse, they are said to be tāmasika. A person living next to a coffee factory looses the ability to enjoy the fragrance of fresh coffee brew. A fishmonger does not even realise that he smells of fish.

10. Colours

Colours and the mind are closely related. Colour tests have shown different personality traits and differences in our nature. Also, universally, the moods and conditions of our minds have been symbolised by colours. Even languages reflect this as in the usage of phrases like 'green with envy' or 'dark mood'. The three mental qualities are symbolised by colours.

Sattva-guṇa: White represents sattva-guṇa which universally stands for peace, purity and brilliance.

Rajo-guṇa: Red is for rajas which stands for characteristics like dynamism and anger. Do recall phrases such as 'seeing red' and 'blood shot eyes'.

Tamo-guṇa: Black is for tamas which indicates inertia, ignorance and sleep.

Please note that these colours are not colours of the skin, but symbolise the moods of the mind. A person with white skin may not be sāttvika nor one with black skin tāmasika.

11. Desires (kāma)

All actions are prompted by desires. Desires spring from a sense of unfulfilment. Even though the sense of unfulfilment is common, our desires can be sāttvika, rājasika or tāmasika depending on what we feel will give us fulfilment.

Sāttvika: Desire to serve others, improve oneself, do good actions, gain knowledge, reach God, search for Truth, be with nature and alleviate others' sorrow are sāttvika. They add beauty to a person. Actions prompted by such desires pave the way for inner unfoldment and sāttvika joy. They are compared to smoke that adds beauty to the fire (dhūmena āvriyate vahniḥ).

Rājasika: Desire for name, fame, wealth, status, power or pleasure are rājasika. The desire to assert, dominate, possess, change others or humble another are also due

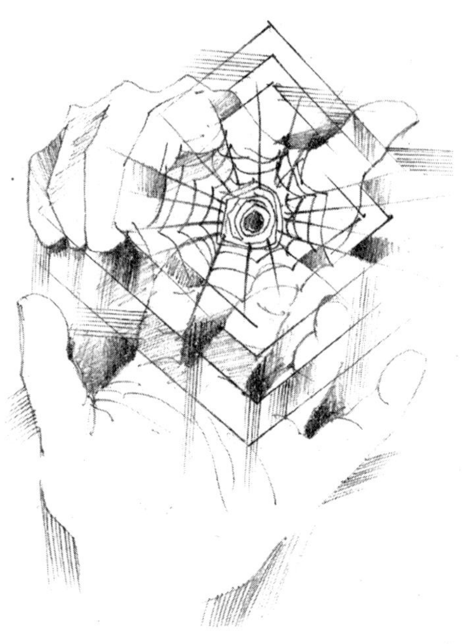

to rajo-guṇa. These cause a lot of stress, strain, restlessness, craving and the drive for competition. They are compared to the dust that covers a mirror (yathā ādarśa malenaca), which prevents us from seeing ourselves as we are. The 'duster' of right attitude and efforts are needed to remove ego-prompted rājasika desires. Rājasika desires do not allow sāttvika desires to bloom within us.

Tāmasika: Desire for inaction, enjoyment without effort, the need to be served and the drive to terrorise or harm others are tāmasika. These make man inactive or criminal- minded. They are compared to the foetus in a womb (yathā ulbena āvṛtam garbhaḥ). It takes a lot of effort, time and pain to get rid of our tāmasika desires. For instance, a person has to go through a hellish time to come out of alcoholism, drug addiction or a record of crime.

12. Faith (śraddhā)

Faith is acceptance of the greatness or nobility of an ideal, cause, object or being, based on an intellectual conviction. Out of that acceptance arises love and respect for the ideal or cause. Thoughts like 'I believe in the existence of God and I know He will protect me', 'I know my Guru is a noble soul and he has my good in his heart', 'I believe that the scriptures are the best guide to life and its problems' and 'I am sure the government will try its best to eradicate corruption' are some examples of faith.

Sāttvika: This faith arises out of a clear and firm intellectual conviction and therefore is unswerving, total and strong. When questioned or tested by oneself or others, it only deepens. For example, when Mīrābāī drank the poison sent by her husband, it turned to nectar. She knew that the Lord's hand is behind everything one gets in life and

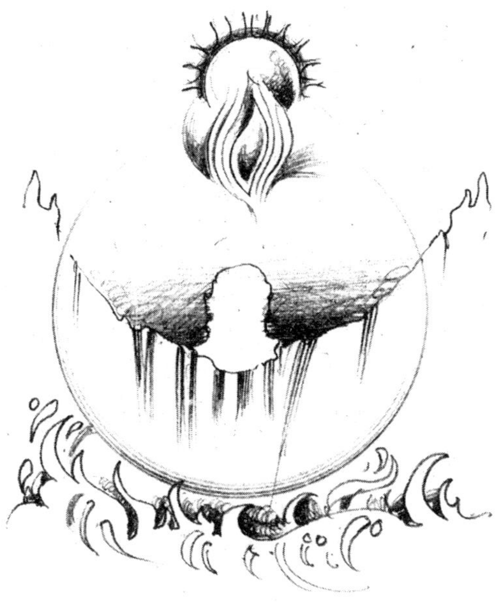

that He is supremely compassionate and shall always take care of His devotees. Sāttvika faith is capable of moving mountains, of manifesting the Lord, of making one realise the Truth and achieve one's goal.

Rājasika: Since this faith is not based on total intellectual conviction, it is partial, vague, inconclusive and doubt ridden. For instance, 'I know God is there, but will he help me?' or 'I doubt if I can ever be successful in life.' Doubts destroy faith and make one fearful and unhappy. For example, life is hell for a person who doubts the fidelity of his or her spouse. Doubts creep into rājasika faith when questioned or tested by oneself or others. If this faith breaks when tested, then cynicism and more doubt sets in.

Tāmasika: This faith is based on sentimental beliefs, emotional upsurges or a result of mass belief. It is therefore blind and makes a person superstitious, fanatic, stubborn and small-minded. A person with blind belief dare not allow his belief to be questioned out of fear of breaking it. Also, he may not even feel a need to question it. In case it breaks when questioned or tested, the person gets shattered and disillusioned. For example, 'If God was there, my son would not have died. I don't believe in Him anymore.' Galileo made a scientific statement that the earth was round which was against the belief of the church. Tāmasika faith of the church authorities prompted then to send Galileo to the gallows.

13. Food (āhāra)

Food is one of the basic necessities of life without which we cannot survive. The food that we eat is divided into three parts. The grossest part is removed from the body by the excretory system. The subtler part goes to form the skin, bones, blood and flesh. The subtlest part forms the mind. Hence, food and the mind are very closely related. The type of food one likes depends on the quality of one's mind, and the quality of the mind, in turn, depends on the quality of one's food. For instance, a sāttvika person likes sāttvika food and the sāttvika food in turn, helps to make the mind more sāttvika. Food is one of the important factors that affect the mind.

Sāttvika: A sāttvika person eats an appropriate quantity of food at regular times and in an unhurried and neat manner. He is careful with regard to what he eats as he is aware of its effect on his body and mind.

Food is sāttvika when it is bought by money earned through righteous means (artha or dhana śuddhi), cooked by a person with good thoughts in hygienic surroundings, served lovingly and aesthetically and eaten with a calm mind. The food itself is juicy and wholesome, nutritious, pleasing to the eye, fragrant, well cooked, filling and fulfilling. Such food increases our life span, makes the mind sharp and alert, helps to maintain a good memory, purifies the mind, strengthens the body, gives us a sense of well being and makes us happy. Examples are fruits, milk, vegetables, pulses and ghee.

Rājasika: A rājasika person eats irregularly or hurriedly, standing or walking, sometimes indulging, sometimes under-eating. He eats to please his tongue, uncaring about its effect on his body and mind. Food becomes rājasika when it is cooked by one with a money motive, served by one who is angry or eaten in a bad mood. Rājasika food is too spicy, too sour, too oily, too hot, too dry, burnt, undercooked or overcooked. Such food causes diseases, agitation in the mind and weakens the body. Examples of rājasika food are junk food, fast food, hotel food and wedding feasts.

Tāmasika: A tāmasika person overeats, or eats irregularly, in a lethargic manner, untidily or while lying down. Food which is stale, tasteless, without nutrition, foul smelling, in the form of leftovers or is not pleasing to look at is tāmasika. Such food increases tāmasika qualities like laziness, inertia, forgetfulness, criminal tendencies and destroys one's health. Some examples are alcohol, meat, garlic and onions.

14. Ideals

All of us have ideals and we idolise a person who exemplifies our ideals or a cause that personifies them. Prompted by our ideals we become what we idolise, as we are influenced by and change in the mould of our idols. What we respect, revere, idolise or worship reflects our qualities and our qualities, in turn, reflect what we idolise.

Sāttvika: A sāttvika person reveres the great, exalted and the noble. He respects good qualities in others, follows the words of the wise, surrenders to noble causes and dedicates his life to them. He follows the footsteps of the great and turns to them for inspiration and strength. For instance, from his childhood, Śivājī wanted to establish Rāma-rājya after listening to the *Rāmāyaṇa*. Such people worship saints, great leaders, God and the scriptures.

Rājasika: A rājasika person reveres the rich, famous, glamorous, powerful and

those in high positions. He copies them in his behaviour and lifestyle and feels honoured to be recognised by such people. He seeks their company and tries to impress them. Such people worship rock stars, sportsmen, politicians, celebrities and stars in glamourous fields.

Tāmasika: The tāmasika person reveres the criminal, the vulgar, terrible, mighty and the cheap. He invokes negative forces and worships ghosts, dictators or smugglers. He also justifies and glorifies terrorists or perverted ideals.

15. Charity (dāna)

Charity is to give money, material, knowledge or time to the needy, to extend a helping hand to those who are less privileged than us, to distribute our excess wealth to those in need or to share what we have with others. The attitude with which one gives makes it sāttvika, rājasika or tāmasika.

Sāttvika: Sāttvika charity is to give out of compassion, a desire to share, a need to help, a sense of duty towards society or being motivated by the sheer joy of giving. Sāttvika charity is given with faith in the cause supported, with modesty and generosity, promptly and when needed, to the right people at the right time, for noble causes and with humility. The receiver is given due respect while giving and one feels privileged for being given a chance to serve and help others. Such an attitude gives a sense of fulfilment, purifies the mind, reduces our sense of possession towards objects, corrects our attitude towards hoarding and increases our compassion and sensitivity towards others.

Rājasika: Rājasika charity is to give after being asked or when forced to give. Many allow themselves to be pressurised into giving donations for charity shows. Some give with a selfish motive of expectation of future repayment or to maintain the goodwill of another. Examples are tipping servants, postmen etc. during Diwali and Holi. Some only make promises or generously offer lip service. Some give to gain publicity, power or position. Others give what is extra, useless or after being reminded many times. Some give little but talk of it endlessly. A rājasika person gives and regrets, gives with the pain of loss, gives out of compulsion or is miserly

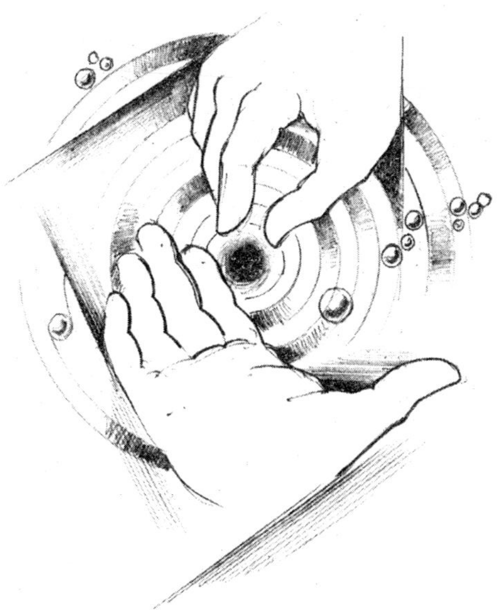

in giving. He therefore does not gain the true joy and fulfilment of giving.

Tāmasika: Tāmasika charity is to give to undeserving or ignoble causes such as giving cigarettes to a poor friend. A tāmasika person may give things which are useless to him or prove unusable or useless to the receiver, like winter clothes to children in the tropics. He or she disrespects, insults, scorns, makes fun of or looks down upon the receiver. He or she ignores all etiquette in giving. Such giving is not born from compassion or sensitivity nor does it foster these qualities – it is not even called a meritorious act (puṇyam).

16. Renunciation (tyāga)

From our childhood we have learned to acquire, hold on, collect and achieve. We are respected, awarded and acknowledged for acquiring wealth, degrees and position. But, in life, we also need the ability to give up, sacrifice or renounce. Renunciation is subtler than acquisition and requires great inner strength. The attitude behind renunciation can be sāttvika, rājasika or tāmasika.

Sāttvika: Sāttvika renunciation is the ability to give up or surrender one's life, possessions, relations or wealth for the sake of a noble cause. Moving examples are soldiers dying for their country, or a spiritual seeker leaving his or her home in search of Truth. Sāttvika renunciation is the giving up of one's attachments to objects, actions, beings and circumstances and performing actions without any expectations. For example, when a saint saw his hermitage burning, he remarked, 'It will make dying easier.'

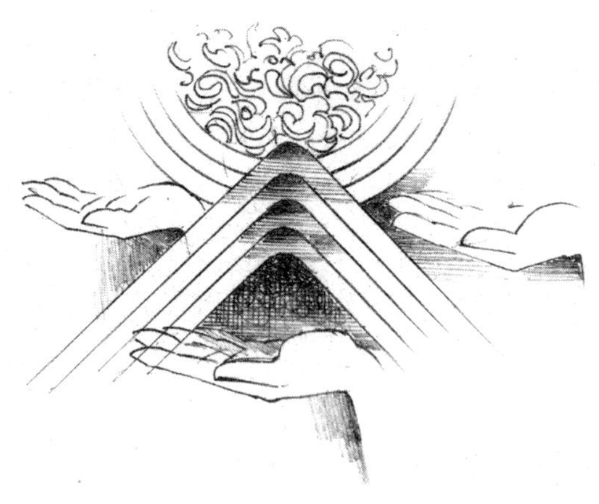

Rājasika: Rājasika renunciation is when giving up is extremely painful and difficult, but one is forced to do so like having to give up smoking for medical reasons. Abandoning one's duties or any undertaking if it is difficult or because of obstacles is rājasika renunciation. To be pained and therefore give up a pursuit or relationship, such as divorce, is also rājasika, unless the circumstances are extreme or when survival necessitates it. To give up an object or relationship out of selfishness, for name and fame in society or in shame is rājasika. For instance this is seen when a politician announces his retirement to gain greater publicity so that he can later say that he came back due to popular demand or when a person resigns from a job as he is forced to do so or to avoid the humility of being fired. Changing one's religion out of monetary considerations also falls under this type.

Tāmasika: Tāmasika renunciation is to give up without thinking, impulsively, indiscriminately, out of strong emotions or by imitating others. Examples are abandoning one's culture for the glamour of another, giving up spiritual practices because there is no compulsion from within or without, giving up one's duties due to laziness or becoming a renunciate to escape household responsibilities.

17. Results hereafter (gati)

Every action has an equal and opposite reaction – 'As we sow, so we reap.' The results of mental, verbal, or physical actions are:

a) The joy or sorrow that we experience while doing the action. For example, I feel happy when I help another person.

b) The impression (vāsanā), good or bad, that it leaves within me. For example, helping another creates a sāttvika vāsanā, addiction deepens a tāmasika vāsanā and so on.

c) The outer results that we get in terms of circumstances, fructify in their own time. Some results of action accrue immediately, others may fructify after a few years and yet others after several lifetimes. For instance, abusing a person may bring instant retaliation or may result in him seeking revenge in some way years later.

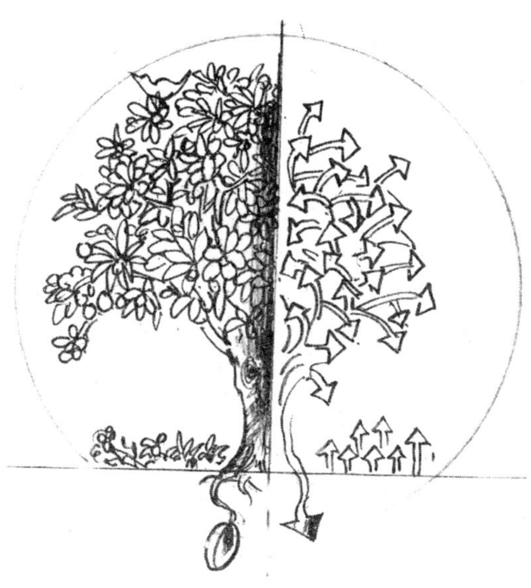

During our lifetime, we enjoy or suffer the results of actions done in our past and present lives. All these also create impressions (vāsanās) in our minds. At the time of death, our predominant vāsanās are drawn from the sum total of our lifetimes of actions and results. These predominant qualities determine the type of body (yathā vṛtti tathā ākṛti) and the field of experience (ante yā mati, sā gati) we will gain hereafter.

Sāttvika: At the time of death a predominantly sāttvika mind goes on to gain the highly subtle body of a presiding deity (devatā) and enjoys subtle fields of experiences such as different types of heavens (lokas). Or he may be born as a human being and enjoy a high standard of living or gain a sāttvika environment in which his sāttvika vāsanās are further fulfilled.

Rājasika: A predominantly rājasika mind at the time of death gets to manifest as a human being in an action oriented environment where he can exhaust his vāsanās of indulgence and activity.

Tāmasika: A person with predominantly tāmasika vāsanās at the time of death manifests as a human being in an inert or evil environment or as some form of animal or plant where he can exhaust his vāsanās of inertia and live in a state of non-thinking. If he has highly criminal vāsanās then he becomes a demon (asura) or may go to various kinds of hell (narakas) where he suffers for his evil deeds.

18. Talk

How and when we talk reflects the state of our mind.

Sāttvika: A sāttvika person thinks and talks. His words are gentle, kind, truthful, well meaning and appropriate. One in a sāttvika mood talks about concepts, noble thoughts, elevating experiences or subtle subjects, like satsaṅga. He questions and discusses to arrive at the truths of a matter (saṁvāda and vāda) through discussions rather than arguments.

Rājasika: A rājasika person either talks too much or in haste. His words are often manipulative, flattering or meant to impress. One in a rājasika mood talks about events, enjoyments, one's own glory or revels in the criticism of others. He argues about issues to prove himself right or to prove others wrong (vivāda or vitaṇḍa vāda).

Tāmasika: A tāmasika person speaks without thinking. His words may be harsh, irresponsible, mean or cruel. He may even use abusive language or curse. One in a tāmasika mood backbites, gossips, pulls down or makes fun of others in a demeaning manner.

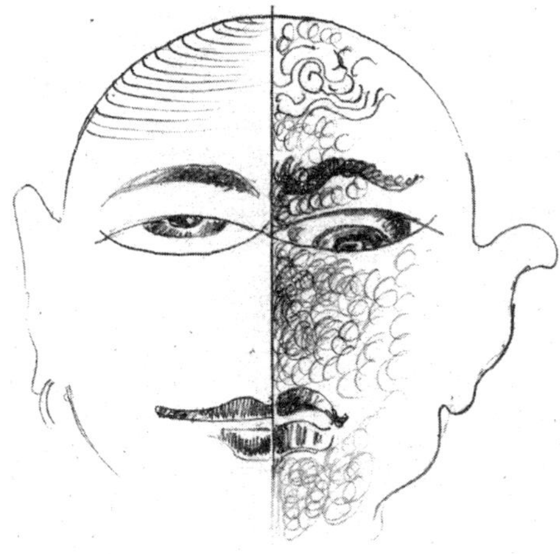

19. Life and Lifestyles

The lifestyle of a person reflects his inner qualities.

Sāttvika: Such a lifestyle is natural and elevating. Those who adopt this lifestyle may follow the principle of simple living and high thinking, like Mahātmā Gandhi who chose to travel by third class so that he could see how the majority in India lived. He had a few, bare necessities and shunned luxury. Some others may have a high standard of living but also enjoy high thinking. Such people do not get attached to comforts and can live without them if required, like Śrī Rāma who even though born in the lap of luxury could renounce it all on a matter of principles. Others have simple thinking and simple living. Many in rural India still lead a simple and pure life. Such people are cheerful, friendly, spontaneous and uncomplicated. A sāttvika life is an inspired and inspiring one.

Rājasika: This lifestyle is quite an artificial one, as superficial or selfish thinking guides its high standard. A Hollywood actress said, 'Deep down I am superficial.' The pace of life is fast, and time flies in activity, pleasures and comforts. Those belonging to this lifestyle strive hard to earn enough to maintain their high standard of living. They are in constant competition with others to acquire and enjoy. As a result, such a lifestyle makes life complicated, the mind agitated and the body exhausted. A rājasika life is either mechanical and filled with drudgery and high pressure at work or pleasure-seeking and selfish.

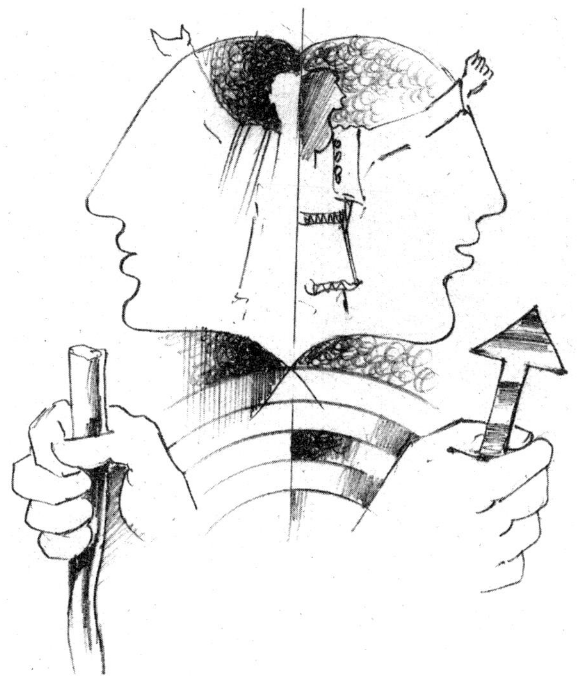

Tāmasika: This refers to a self-destructive lifestyle that can also cause harm to others. Such people either live without thinking or resort to destructive thinking. They waste their time in unproductive occupations or self-destructive activities like addictions which often makes them paupers. Even if they gain financially, the wealth they amass through criminal activities is also spent in unhealthy ways. A tāmasika life is uninspired and ignoble and those who adopt this lifestyle lose the wonderful opportunity of a human birth to uplift themselves.

20 Awareness

In the ladder of evolution, the greater the awareness and sensitivity, the more evolved the being. Therefore, we see that plants are more aware than inert objects, animals more than plants and man much more aware and sensitive than animals. The degree of awareness or sensitivity depends on our inner qualities.

Sāttvika: A sāttvika person is a highly aware and sensitive being. He is aware of his own body and mind, sensitive to his immediate surroundings and appreciates his relationship with the entire universe, God or the Totality. He lives in harmony with all, cares about others and therefore serves all. He is a highly refined being (saṁskṛta puruṣa) and is called a 'man-man' as his actions are humane. When a sāttvika person evolves to directly experience the universal Truth, he is called a 'God-man', a divine being, such as Śrī Buddha or Swami Vivekananda.

Rājasika: A rājasika person is most aware of himself and his own needs. Even when he is aware of the needs of others, he is too selfish to care and therefore does little for others.

Such people feel that the whole world is meant only for their enjoyment. They believe that life is for the epicurean purpose of 'eat, drink and be merry' and all their energies are spent in doing just that. Such a one is called vikṛta puruṣa or 'animal-man', as his awareness level is limited.

Tāmasika: A tāmasika person is unaware of himself or others and therefore has no idea or vision of the totality or his relation with it. He therefore cares little beyond his basic creature comforts and survival. Such a person is called prākṛta puruṣa or 'plant-man' or 'stone-man', as his awareness level is very low.

The Guṇa Chart

A check list of 23 aspects to make ourselves Just Right

	Aspect	(Sāttvika) Sattva-guṇa dominant 'Just right'	(Rājasika) Rajo-guṇa dominant 'Too tight'	(Tāmasika) Tamo-guṇa dominant 'Too loose'
1.	Vision (dṛṣṭi) (Page 9)	Holistic, unifying (abheda dṛṣṭi)	Partial, divisive (bheda dṛṣṭi)	Narrow, blind (alpa dṛṣṭi)
2.	Actions-undertaking (Karma) (Page 15)	Plan out work and work out plan	Incomplete planning	No planning
3.	Actions – inherent tendencies (Page 19)	According to one's inherent tendencies (svadharma) Joy in action	Not according to inherent tendencies (paradharma) Joy in results	According to one's lower tendencies (adharma) Joy in inaction or wrong actions

	Aspect	(Sāttvika) Sattva-guṇa dominant 'Just right'	(Rājasika) Rajo-guṇa dominant 'Too tight'	(Tāmasika) Tamo-guṇa dominant 'Too loose'
4.	Action – duties (kartavya) (Page 19)	Duties done cheerfully	Duties done with tension or as a burden	Duties not done
5.	Intellect (buddhi) (Page 26)	Understands what to do	Confused about what to do	Does not understand or misunderstands
6.	Patience and Will (dhṛti) (Page 31)	Under all circumstances	Under particular circumstances	Holds on to false notions or actions
7.	Efforts	In improving oneself	In changing others	No efforts or wrong efforts
8.	Happiness (sukha) (Page 36)	In subtle pursuits cheerful, lasting joy	In gross pursuits Exciting, momentary joy	In low pursuits Dull, base joy

	Aspect	(Sāttvika) Sattva-guṇa dominant 'Just right'	(Rājasika) Rajo-guṇa dominant 'Too tight'	(Tāmasika) Tamo-guṇa dominant 'Too loose'
9.	Sleep (Page 41)	Deep and sound	Restless and interrupted	Heavy
10.	Powers of mind (Page 43)	Discrimination (viveka śakti)	Projection (vikṣepa śakti)	Veiling (āvaraṇa śakti)
11.	Sense Organs (indriya) (Page 46)	Keen and sensitive	Tired or strained	Dull
12.	Colours (Page 49)	White (and gentle colours)	Red (and gaudy colours)	Black (and dark colours)
13.	Desires (kāma) (Page 51)	Noble, selfless	For name, pleasure, power selfish	For inaction, harmful

	Aspect	(Sāttvika) Sattva-guṇa dominant 'Just right'	(Rājasika) Rajo-guṇa dominant 'Too tight'	(Tāmasika) Tamo-guṇa dominant 'Too loose'
14.	Faith (śraddhā) (Page 54)	Firm and unswerving	Ridden with doubts	Blind and superstitious
15.	Food (āhāra) (Page 58)	Wholesome	Spicy and junk	Harmful or bad
16.	Ideals (Page 62)	Great	Powerful and glamorous	Criminal and vulgar
17.	Charity (dāna) (Page 65)	Give without expectation and pride Generous, joyful	Give with expectation and pride Miserly, with pain	Give indiscriminately Insulting

	Aspect	(Sāttvika) Sattva-guṇa dominant 'Just right'	(Rājasika) Rajo-guṇa dominant 'Too tight'	(Tāmasika) Tamo-guṇa dominant 'Too loose'
18.	Renunciation (tyāga) (Page 69)	Give up bad qualities	Give up objects or beings in and with pain	Give up indiscriminately
19.	Results hereafter (gati) (Page 73)	Subtle field of experience (svarga) Deity (devatā) or noble human birth	Gross field experience (pṛthivī) Action oriented human birth	Pain- filled field of experience (naraka) Animal, plant birth, demon (asura) or low human birth
20.	Talk (Page 77)	Concepts Discussion	Events Arguments	People Opinions

	Aspect	(Sāttvika) Sattva-guṇa dominant 'Just right'	(Rājasika) Rajo-guṇa dominant 'Too tight'	(Tāmasika) Tamo-guṇa dominant 'Too loose'
21.	Life (Page 79)	Inspired and inspiring	Glamorous and fast, Competitive and high pressured	Ignoble and wasteful
22.	Lifestyle (Page 79)	Natural, simple living high thinking	Artificial and fast life, superficial thinking	Surviving, no thinking or wrong thinking
23.	Awareness (Page 82)	Aware, care and dare (Saṁskṛta puruṣa) Man-man / God-man	Aware but does not care (Vikṛta puruṣa) Animal-man	Unaware, does not care (Prākṛta puruṣa) Plant-man / Stone-man

In Conclusion – Tuning the Mind

The strings of our mind should not be 'too loose' nor 'too tight', but 'just right'. Our mind should be sattva-dominant. Suppose by birth or during the course of life one is rajas or tamas dominant, how can he overcome his inherent or inherited negative qualities (vāsanās)? Here are a few tips to help us tune our minds.

1. By being intellectually alert: Objective and alert observation of one's thought flow and behaviour makes us more aware of ourselves. We should recognise the sāttvika, rājasika or tāmasika tendencies in us and avoid self-condemnation, justification, pretending not to see them or hiding from what we see of ourselves. Rather, we should accept them. This 'choiceless awareness' gives us an insight into the working of our mind and hastens the process of cleansing it and tuning it up.

2. By analysis: A doctor examines a patient, diagnoses the disease, understands the factors that aggravate the symptoms and then suggests a cure. Similarly, we must analyse how sāttvika, rājasika or tāmasika thoughts

arise, what sustains, aggravates and stops them. When we realise that by brooding over desired objects we only increase the intensity of desires within us, we should avoid such unhealthy thinking. We should also avoid rājasika or tāmasika company whenever possible, seek the company of sāttvika people, read literature that encourages noble thoughts in us and entertain our minds with sāttvika pursuits. For instance, a person trying to overcome alcoholism is advised to avoid visiting liquor bars and the company of those who have a similar tendency and asked to take up an indoor or outdoor sport.

3. By substitution: When a person grows tired of hearing the same hard rock music every day, he retapes the same cassettes with some other music. Similarly, harmful rājasika and tāmasika tendencies should be substituted with sāttvika tendencies. For example, selfish thoughts should be replaced by selfless thoughts and miserly thoughts with those of generosity. Initially, one may feel strained or think that such an effort is hypocritical or artificial. But, over time, one develops a taste for sāttvika thoughts and with practice, they become a habit. For instance, with persistent practice, Vālmīki's 'marā' became substituted by 'Rāma'.

4. By outgrowing tendencies: Some rājasika and tāmasika tendencies are shed through mental and physical growth, just as we painlessly outgrow our attachments to childhood toys.

5. By observing others: It is always easier to watch others than ourselves. If we can observe others – not judge, condemn or criticise but just observe them – we would understand a great deal about the human mind and behaviour.

This will help us to look within with greater clarity and deal with others and ourselves with greater sensitivity and sympathy. Observing the terrible consequences of certain rājasika and tāmasika tendencies in others removes them from us. For instance, seeing the trauma of a drug addict may remove even a little desire that one may have for experimenting with drugs.

6. By one's own suffering: The wise learn from the experiences of others. If we do not learn from others, then we have to undergo suffering due to some rājasika or tāmasika tendencies. Such suffering, at times, removes our rājasika and tāmasika qualities. A youngster may tend to speed even though he is warned by his own intellect, his parents and the law. But a near accident with a truck or a night in jail for speeding often totally sobers him down.

7. By the path of action (Karma Yoga): Doing the right action with the right attitude and receiving results with the right attitude exhausts our existing negative qualities and prevents new ones from being formed. What is right action with right attitude? Doing one's duties or actions in tune with our positive inherent tendencies with dedication to a noble cause, without ego and egocentric desires is right action with right attitude. This is called 'iśvara-arpaṇa-buddhi' – the attitude of dedication to the Lord.

What is meant by receiving results with the right attitude? To be able to accept all results with cheer, without cursing, complaining or increasing likes, dislikes or reactions is called prasāda-buddhi – the attitude of cheerful acceptance. For example, temple prasādam, even if found to be not too tasty, is eaten with an attitude of cheerful acceptance.

Also, when it is tasty, it is shared with as many as possible, even with strangers.

In short, in Swami Chinmayanandajī's words, "What we do with what we have is our gift to Him. What we get back is His gift to us."

8. By the path of devotion (Bhakti Yoga): Attachment to the Divine liberates us from rājasika and tāmasika tendencies, just as love for the form of the Lord reduces our attachment to our own body.

9. By the path of Knowledge (Jñāna Yoga): By inquiry into what is real and unreal, eternal and ephemeral, we can get rid of rājasika and tāmasika tendencies. We may question, 'Who am I? What is the ultimate goal of my life? What is the real source of happiness – objects or the Self? Is there anything eternal in this ever-changing world?' and so on. Such enquiry has to be undertaken with a very subtle mind, which results in it becoming finely tuned.

10. By the path of meditation (Dhyāna Yoga): During meditation, our dormant and subtler vāsanās spring forth in our awareness. When we witness them without involvement, they vanish by themselves.

11. Sequentially: Tamo-guṇa cannot be overcome by tamo-guṇa – laziness is not overcome by remaining lazy or sleeping. Certain tāmasika characteristics cannot be overcome by directly substituting them with sattva-guṇa just as a lazy person will not be able to start doing noble actions all of a sudden. He will initially have to resort to some rājasika form of activity which could, in time, be replaced by sāttvika ones. The progression is from laziness to activity, and then to selfless activity.

12. By doing spiritual practices: Spiritual practices like pūjā (worshipping the form of the Lord), japa (repetition of the name of the Lord), prāṇāyāma (breath-regulation), svādhyāya (studying the scriptures), pārāyaṇa (chanting the scriptures) and dhyāna (meditation) are time-tested and very effective means of tuning the mind. There are many more ways that we can discover of tuning and fine-tuning our mind.

Dear Reader,
I pray that this book inspires you to fine-tune yourself after which life will become one grand spontaneous performance.
May you receive a standing ovation from the world!